BLACKWELL'S LEARNING LIBRARY No. 80

Edited by John Cutforth and J. C. Gagg

ARMS AND ARMOUR

by

J. N. T. VINCE

Illustrations by David C. Wray

BASIL BLACKWELL OXFORD

First published 1975

0 631 13250 3

Author's Note

I should like to acknowledge the help I received from the following:
The Director, the British Museum; C. J. T. Vince; C. N. Gowing, M.A., F.M.A., Curator, Buckinghamshire County Museum; The Master of the Armouries, Her Majesty's Tower of London.

CONTENTS

In a cricket match some players (the batsmen and the wicket keeper) wear pads and gloves to protect them from the hard and fast-moving ball. Footballers, too, often wear pads to protect their shins from an accidental kick.

Racing drivers and horsemen wear crash helmets in case they have an accident. Rugby players wear scrum caps to protect their ears.

All these things worn by sportsmen are rather like the armour soldiers used long ago when they went into battle.

When the first man threw a stone at his enemy, or tried to hit him with a stick, the need for armour of some sort became important. Shields were perhaps the first things to be used, and helmets have been worn by warriors for thousands of years. Even today's soldiers wear helmets.

Men used to fight with sticks, stones, axes, swords, spears, bows and arrows. These were the things their shields and helmets protected them against, and they also began to wear special dress on their bodies.

This book describes some of the weapons and armour used at different times in the past.

THE FIRST WEAPONS

Long ago men hunted animals for food. They used rocks and sticks, and later bows and arrows. When such things are used to hurt or kill another creature they are called weapons. Almost anything can become a weapon. Many people use a rolled-up newspaper to swat a wasp. When men began to quarrel with one another they used hunting weapons in their battles. Objects such as stone axes or hammers which were used to chop wood or knock posts into the ground could also become the tools of war.

Stone

A hard kind of stone called flint was used long ago to make tools and weapons. Its edges could be very sharp. Two large flints

Part of the Bayeux Tapestry

German soldiers of about 1525

were banged together so that small flakes kept breaking off each one, and in this way they were shaped to form axe heads and spear heads. It took a long time to make one of these stone weapons.

After a stone head had been made it was fixed to a wooden handle. Long strips of leather were bound tightly around the handle to keep the stone head in place.

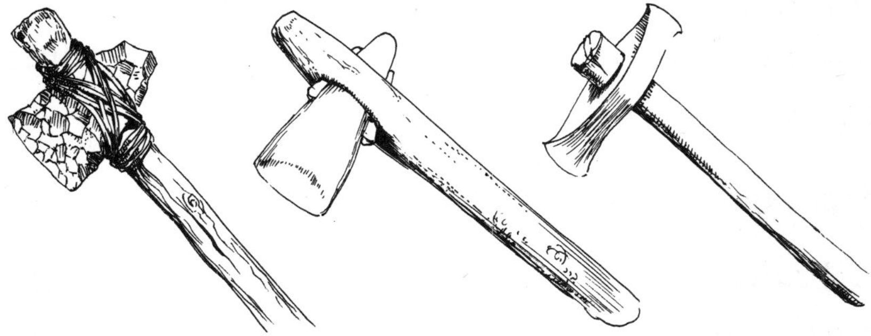

Look at the three stone axes. The middle axe head is not fixed with leather strips, but is wedged in a hole at the top of the handle. How would you describe the other axe in the picture?

These stone weapons were made by men who lived a long time ago. We now call them the Stone Age men.

Men who lived in the Stone Age built very simple huts to live in. Their homes have vanished but we can still find some of the work they did. At Avebury and Stonehenge there are two great stone circles which we think were used for worship. There are many smaller stone circles in the British Isles. If you live near a stone circle try to visit it and find out when it was made.

Bronze and Iron

Long after the first stone weapons were made men found out how to make metal weapons. They discovered how to melt copper and tin, then by mixing these together they made another metal called bronze.

Men usually made bronze weapons in

moulds, shaped like the weapon they needed.

The metal was melted and poured into the mould, and when it had cooled the weapon was taken out. It was then polished and sharpened. Bronze could also be beaten into shape without being heated in a fire.

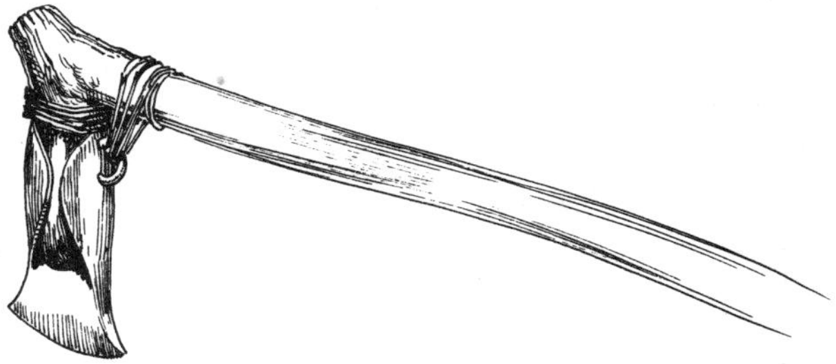

Above is a picture of a bronze axe. There is a groove on each side of the axe head, and the handle fits into these grooves. The handle is tightly bound with leather, while another strip of leather is fixed through the small hole in the head. A leather strip was also used to fix the bronze spearhead to its shaft.

This axe has a hole in the back of the head where the handle fits.

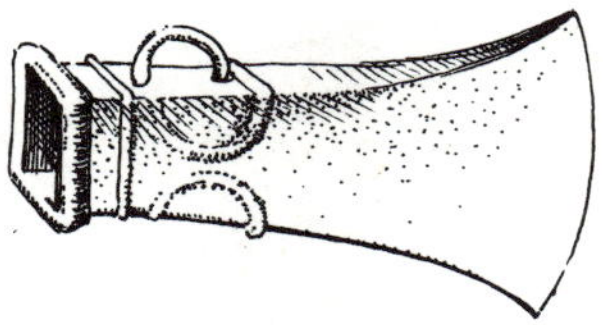

Men who made bronze weapons did not know how to make swords, but they made long knives called *rapiers*. Here is a picture of a bronze rapier. The blade was about 50 centimetres long, and the handle was made of horn or wood. When the handle and blade were fitted together rivets were placed in each hole. These rivets fixed the two parts together.

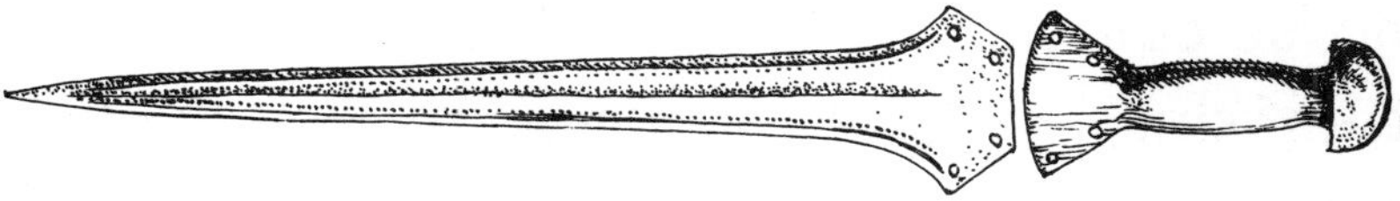

After a long time men discovered how to make iron. It is harder than bronze so men began to use it instead of bronze. To make iron, special rock was melted in ovens until the metal in the rock changed into a liquid. This liquid was allowed to run into a narrow mould. When it cooled it became a solid bar of iron. Then the blacksmith could use it to make into all kinds of tools, weapons or other useful objects.

Men who lived in the Iron Age liked to live on hilltops. They made a deep ditch around their village and at the top of the ditch they built a strong wooden fence. Today we often call these hill-top villages "hill forts". There is a famous hill fort near Uffington between Faringdon and Wantage. On the steep hillside close by there is a large figure of a horse cut into the chalk. Some people think that this horse was carved in the chalk to mark the place where an important battle took place a very long time ago.

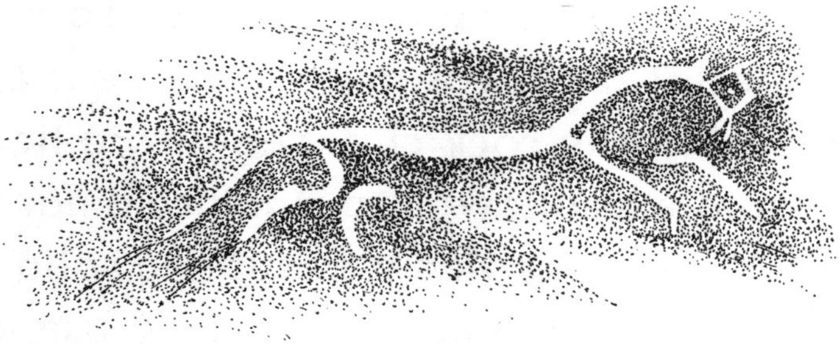

THE ROMANS

Roman soldiers came to Britain with Julius Caesar as their leader. In the picture below you can see a standard bearer, two Roman officers and a legionary.

One officer is carrying a round shield and his body is protected by a metal breast plate. The standard bearer is wearing a shirt made of leather. Pieces of metal are sewn to the shirt so that it looks as if it is covered with scales like a fish. These metal scales protect the soldier's body, while metal straps protect each shoulder.

Here is a Roman helmet made of metal, with curved pieces at the side to protect the face. Roman soldiers used spears, swords and daggers. Their swords were short with straight blades, and the handles were made of bone or wood.

SAXONS AND DANES

After the Romans left Britain, Saxons and Danes came and settled here. They were fierce fighters, who used round shields made of metal and wood. They protected their heads with round metal helmets. Their swords were short and pointed.

There are pictures of their shield, helmet and arms on page 16.

Look at the Saxon weapons. There are two battle axes and three long spears. The axe heads and spearheads were made of metal, while the handles were made of wood. Spears were about eight feet long (two and a half metres). Measure out how long this is. The weapon like a heavy knife is called a *scramasax*. It, too, has a wooden handle.

Saxon arms and armour

THE NORMANS

Over 900 years ago there was a Saxon king named Harold. He had a quarrel with Duke William of Normandy, who lived in France on the other side of the English Channel. People from Normandy are called Normans.

King Harold and Duke William both wanted to be King of England, and to settle the argument Duke William built many ships and in 1066 sailed across the English Channel with his army. He landed in England and met Harold's army near Hastings in Sussex. There the two armies had a fierce battle.

King Harold was killed and Duke William became King. He had an Abbey built on the spot where Harold fell, and this is now called Battle Abbey. The town which grew up around the Abbey is still called Battle, and the letters posted nowadays near Hastings often bear a special postmark.

Harold was said to have been killed by an arrow in his eye but this may not be true.

We know a lot about the arms and armour in the battle of Hastings because a very large picture was made about the battle and the quarrel with Harold. The picture was embroidered by many ladies. It is known as the "Bayeux Tapestry" and can still be seen in the town of Bayeux in France, but it may have been made in England.

The Bayeux Tapestry is of course very old, since it was made in 1086. In 1966 some special English stamps were made showing some of the figures to be seen on the Bayeux Tapestry.

Next to page 6 is a picture of part of the Tapestry, showing the Norman knights and archers attacking the Saxon army. The knights are riding on horses. You can see

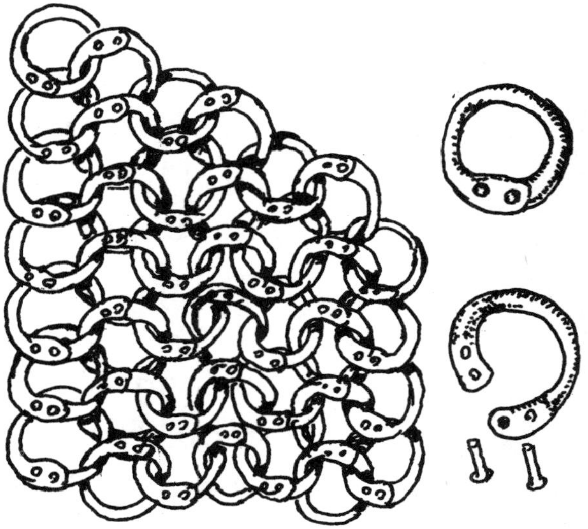

their coats of chain mail, which was made of hundreds of metal rings joined together like chains. A coat of chain mail stretched down to the knees, and men used to wear thick leather jackets underneath. Norman archers used long bows, and carried their arrows in quivers. The quiver was hung on the archer's back with a strong strap.

The picture on the next page also shows the type of armour worn in Norman times. This

picture of a knight was copied from a book written by hand in 1109. The knight has a short sword and a long spear and his body is covered with a long coat of chain mail. The flag fixed to the end of the spear is called a *pennon*. His head is protected by a small cone-shaped helmet. The strip of metal protecting his nose is called a *nasal piece*, and the helmet is held in place with a leather strap.

CRUSADERS

In the days of King Richard I (Richard Lion Heart) many knights travelled to the Holy Land to fight against the Turks. These campaigns were called the "Crusades" or the "Wars of the Cross". Men who fought in them were called Crusaders. What is another name for the Holy Land ? Find this country in an atlas.

The Holy Land is a hot country. To keep the fierce heat of the sun from their chain mail, knights wore long cloth coats called *surcoats*, often decorated with a cross.

Crusaders often travelled on horseback.

You can see two Crusaders on the next page. The first knight is covered from head to foot in a suit of chain mail, and over this he wears a cloth surcoat without sleeves.

He is wearing spurs on his heels. The spurs are long and pointed, and the knight would dig them into his horse's side to make it gallop faster.

The second knight has a round helmet, a belt, and spurs strapped to his feet.

Here are some of the weapons and helmets used by Crusaders.

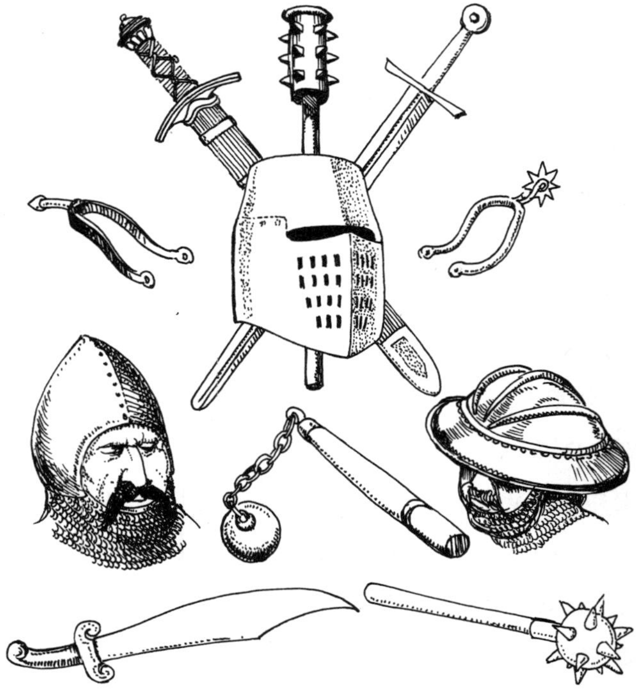

Many knights died in the Crusades and were buried in the Holy Land. Others came back to England and their monuments can still be seen in churches. Try to find some.

PLATE ARMOUR

After chain mail had been in use for a long time men started to use extra armour. The extra pieces were made of metal or boiled leather.

Opposite is a picture of a knight with extra armour. On top of his chain mail he is wearing a leather studded jacket and a metal breast plate. His hands are protected by leather gloves. The top of each leg is guarded with a strip of studded leather, and leather pieces also protect each knee. He wears a sword and a dagger on his swordbelt.

Later all the extra pieces of armour were made from metal sheets, or plates as they were sometimes called. These metal plates were shaped to cover the body, arms, hands, legs, knees and feet. The extra pieces were

fixed on top of the chain mail with leather straps. Armour made from metal plates is called plate armour.

Here is a picture of a knight in plate armour, taken from a brass memorial in a church. His neck and shoulders are still protected by chain mail. He wears a long sword and a dagger.

There are hundreds of brass memorials like these in our parish churches. The lines of the design were cut into the brass plates. You can make an exact copy of a brass figure by making a "rubbing" with a wax crayon and a sheet of paper. Before you make a rubbing it is important to ask permission. Try to find out more about brass rubbing.

Here are two examples of such brass monuments.

FOOT SOLDIERS

When a knight went to fight for the king he took some of his own men with him. Their weapons were sometimes made from the tools they used on the farm.

Knights usually rode on horseback. Ordinary soldiers were called *foot soldiers*, as they fought on foot. One of their most important weapons was the sword. The picture opposite was copied from a very old book which was written, by hand, to show men how to fight with a sword. The small shield held by one man is called a *buckler*.

The men at arms are both wearing suits of mail. Over their mail they are wearing thickly padded coats called *jacks*. These were made from layers of leather or canvas, with

metal discs sewn between the two layers. One of the men here is wearing a jack without sleeves. The name "jacket" comes from the word jack. Both men are wearing plate armour on their legs.

Here are some of the weapons used by foot soldiers.

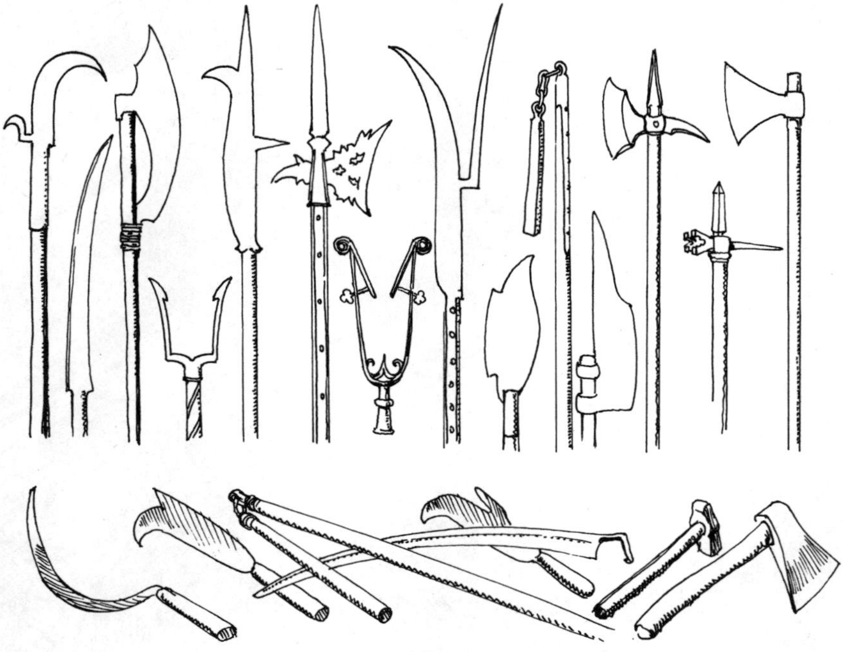

Armourers at work in the 16th century

BOWMEN

Bowmen were very important in the days before gunpowder was used. On page 32 is a picture of a bowman wearing a jack over his chain mail. The stout wooden bow is about 1.8 metres and it is called a longbow. This archer carries his arrows in his belt. The arrows were about three feet long, made of wood with heads made of metal.

Longbowmen could shoot their arrows more than one hundred metres. Some English people still use longbows today for sport. They shoot their arrows at targets.

Longbows were made from the yew, a tree which is harmful to cattle. This may explain why yew trees are so often found in church-yards, away from the cows. Yew trees were grown in every village or town so that there

would be enough wood to make bows.

Here are some metal arrow heads used on the arrows of longbows.

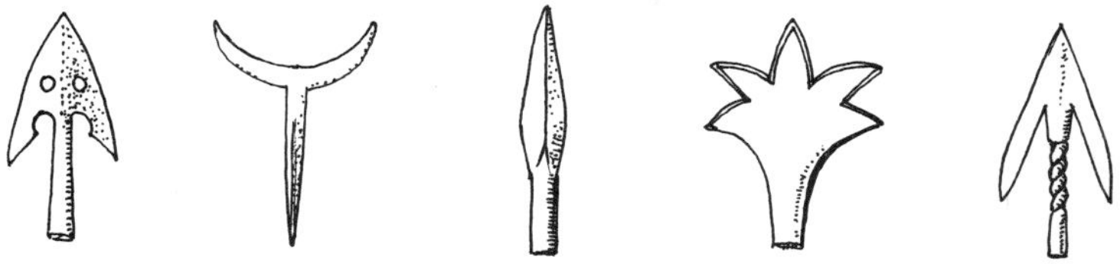

Robin Hood and his followers used longbows. What stories have you read about Robin Hood? Try to find out about other people who used longbows. In some parts of the world they are still used by people who hunt for their food.

Craftsmen who made bows were called bowmakers, and there are still people with the surname Bowmaker. Look for this name in a telephone directory.

CROSSBOWS

Hundreds of years after the longbow had been in use the crossbow was invented. This was made of steel because steel is stronger than wood. Crossbow arrows were called *bolts or quarrels,* and they were about thirty eight cm long. Look at those in the drawing.

You can see two crossbowmen. One is getting ready to shoot and the other has just shot his bolt. Crossbows took longer to load than longbows.

Long ago men had to spend some time each year practising their skill with the longbow or crossbow. The place where the target shooting was held was called the *butts*. A butt was a high bank of earth behind the target to stop stray arrows. If you look

at a map of your town or village the old butts may still be marked.

Longbows and crossbows were also used for hunting.

TOURNAMENTS

When knights were not fighting in real battles they used to practise fighting at tournaments.

Tournaments were usually held in large fields. A wooden wall, about a metre high, was set up across the field and two mounted knights used to charge towards each other from opposite sides of the wall. They pointed their long lances over the wall, and each knight had to try to push the other off his horse.

They used blunt lances so that they would not pierce their opponent's armour. Tournament lances were also very thin so that they would break easily.

At the tournament knights used to wear extra pieces of armour to protect themselves.

A suit of armour could easily weigh about thirty four kg, and if a Knight fell from his horse he was often badly injured.

On pages 38-39 are two knights at a tournament. They are wearing heavy helmets. One knight has struck the other on the head and forced his visor open. The visor is the front part of the helmet which lifts up.

Here are two knights' helmets showing them with the visors both closed and open.

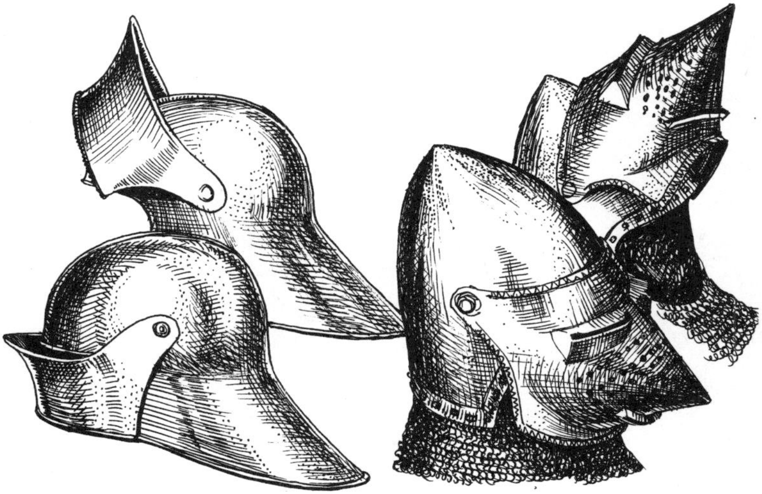

Two knights figh

g at a tournament

Look again at the picture of the two knights at the tournament.

The whole of the knight's body is protected by armour. Each knight carries a shield made of metal or wood and leather. One of the knights in the picture has his shield fixed to his armour, and his left hand is protected by a long steel glove. The knights hold their shields on the left and their lances in their right hands. Even the horses wear armour on their heads and necks.

Men who made armour were called armourers and they were very clever workmen. In the next picture you can see how the armourer fastened the front part of the helmet to the back. This helmet has an extra piece of metal which was screwed on above the visor when the knight went to a tournament. It was called a *tilting piece*. Could the knight raise his visor when the tilting piece was screwed in position? This helmet weighed 5.8 kg.

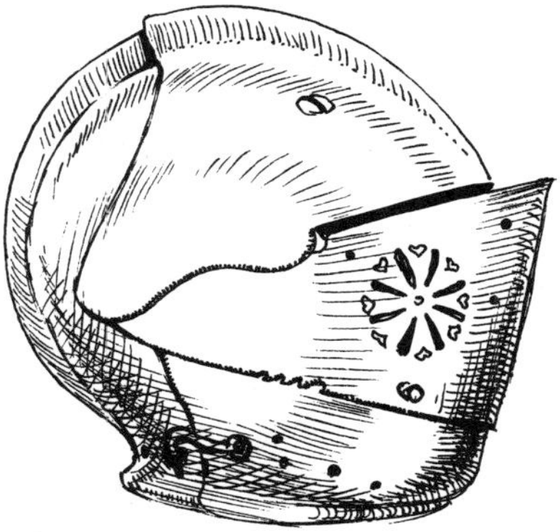

Wearing heavy armour made the knight very hot. The holes, arranged to make a pattern on the visor, allowed the knight to breathe more easily.

The notches on the edge of the visor show how many tournaments the owner has won.

Some helmets had a little door in the side of the visor. The door made it easier for the wearer to breathe. A French king lost his life at a tournament when the door of his helmet came open and he was pierced with a lance. After this, helmets of this sort were not made.

Here is another helmet. The front of the helmet and the visor are held in place with strong clasps and turn-buttons. The wearer looks through the slits in the top of the visor.

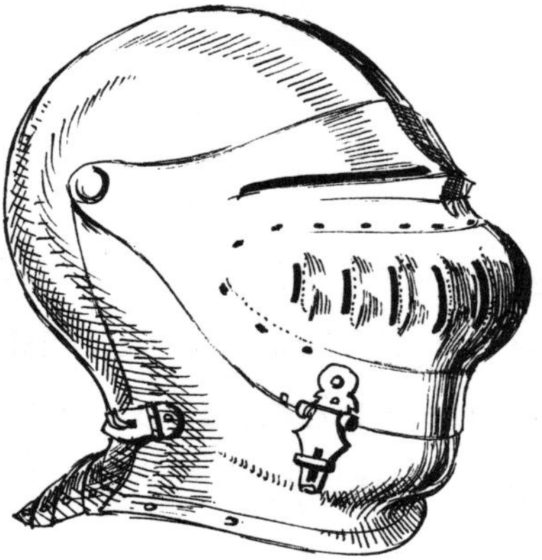

Another important piece of armour was the breast plate which was shaped to protect the chest. This breast plate has an extra piece fixed to the right hand side. It is called a lance rest, and the knight used to rest his lance on it.

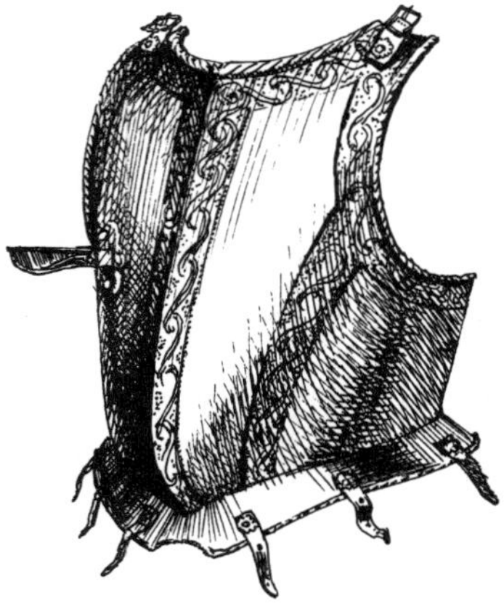

At the tournament the knight protected all his body with armour. Here is a special glove which was worn on the left hand. A glove like this is called a *gauntlet*, and the knight in the picture on pages 38-39 is wearing one.

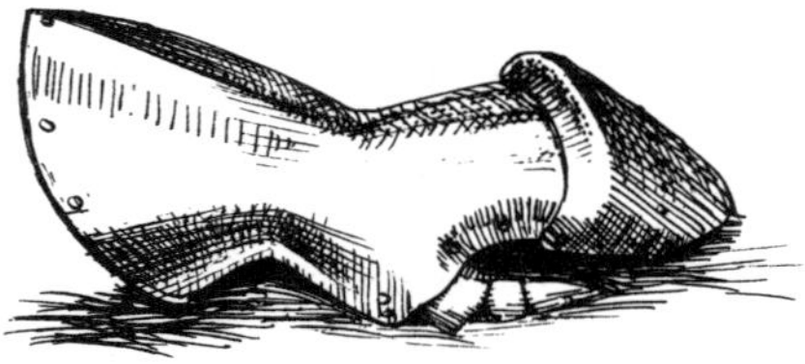

FOOT COMBAT

Not all tournaments took place on horseback. Some tournaments were fought on foot. When a knight fought on foot he sometimes used a very large sword which had to be held with both hands. The blade could be as much as two metres.

Opposite you can see a knight ready for a fight on foot. He has an extra piece of armour on his left shoulder to protect his neck from the swinging blow of a sword or axe. Two more pieces of armour, fixed to the bottom of his breast plate, protect the top of his legs. His hands are protected with gauntlets. He wears a sword which is fixed to his belt. Underneath his plate armour he wears chain mail. His battle axe has a long point and sharp claws.

rear view front view

When a knight fought at a tournament he often wore a short cloth coat over his armour. This coat was decorated with his own special colours and signs, which were called a *coat of arms*. The same colours and signs were displayed on his shield. This enabled him to be easily recognised by his friends and his enemies.

Here is one of these coats.

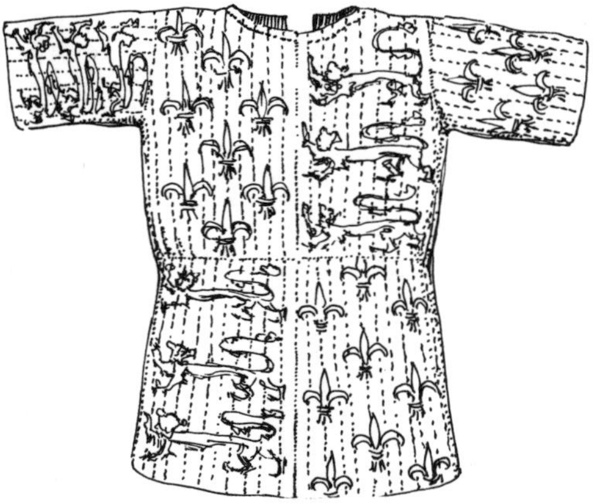

In the coloured picture on the opposite page you can see two coats of arms and two shields.

HENRY VIII

Here is a suit of armour made for King Henry VIII, who was a big man. You can still see his armour in the Tower of London.

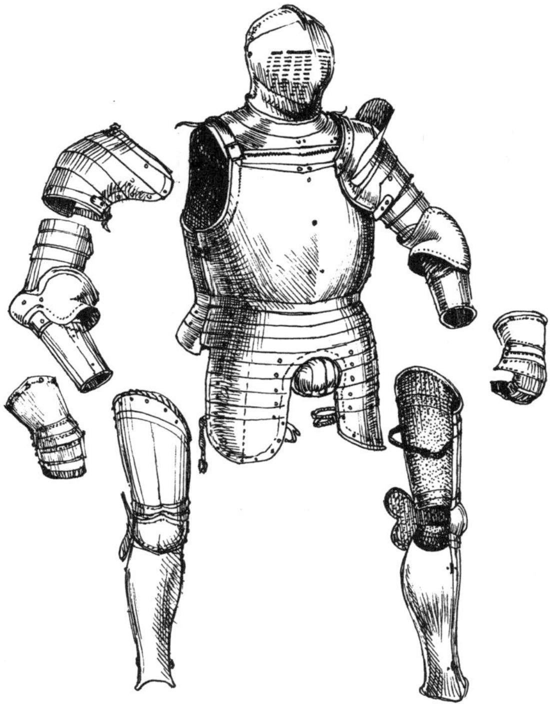

ELIZABETHAN ARMOUR

Queen Elizabeth I was one of Henry VIII's daughters. Opposite is a picture of an Elizabethan gentleman in his armour. It does not look the same as the armour worn by Henry VIII. The breast plate which protects the wearer's chest has a pointed lower edge. It has a lance rest like the one on page 43. His neck is protected by a gorget. On his left hand he wears a gauntlet. In his right hand he holds a lance. Find all these things in the picture.

Elizabethan armourers liked to decorate their armour with patterns. On page 50 are some Elizabethan helmets. The armourers decorated helmets with patterns engraved on the metal. The armour shown opposite has the same pattern from head to toe.

49

These are Elizabethan helmets.

Swords and daggers were still important weapons in the reign of Elizabeth I. Men who made swords were called swordsmiths. The handle of a sword is called the *hilt*, and the small knob at the top of the handle is called the *pommel*. Elizabethan swordsmiths added extra pieces of metal to the hilt to guard the swordsman's hand.

Here are two Elizabethan sword hilts.

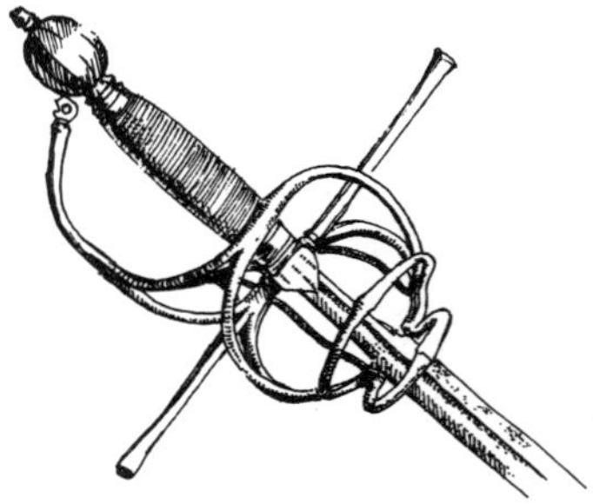

Below is a drawing of an Elizabethan dagger. Queen Elizabeth I made a law about daggers which said that no one was allowed to use or make a dagger more than 30 cm long. During Elizabeth I's reign daggers were made with the cross piece curved downwards. Daggers made in this way looked like a letter E.

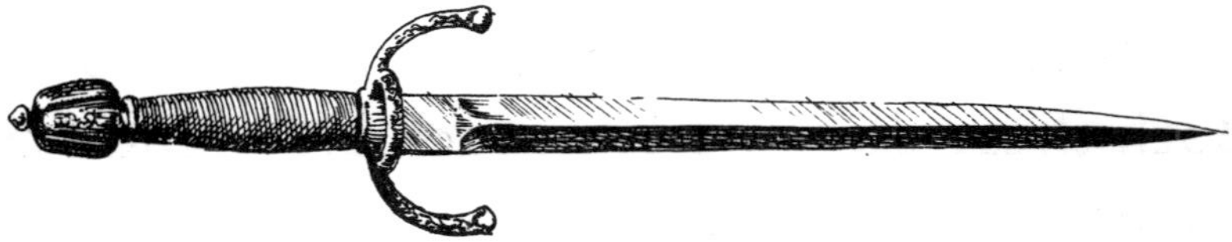

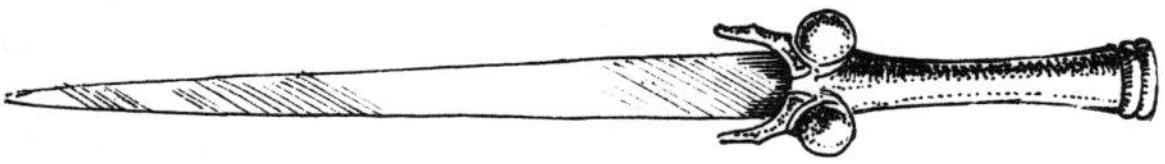

Here are two more daggers with special names. The dagger at the top is called a *rondel dagger*. It has a round disc at both the top and the bottom of the handle. The handle is made of wood and bound with strands of wire. The other dagger is called a *ballock dagger*. The hilt of this dagger is like two small balls, and the handle is made of bone. Both these daggers are much older than the Elizabethan dagger.

THE CIVIL WAR (1642–1651)

King Charles I had an argument with his Parliament, and his army fought many battles with Parliament's army. We call the troubled times of Charles I the Civil War. When Charles I was captured he was put on trial and sentenced to be beheaded. His execution took place in Whitehall, London on 30th January 1649.

King Charles's followers were called Cavaliers. Some of the Parliamentarians had their hair cut short, so the Cavaliers called them Roundheads or Cropheads.

You can see a picture of Civil War armour on pages 54 and 55. The cavalryman (horseman) wears a heavy helmet called a *lobster tail*, with metal bars to protect his face. His cheeks are protected by metal plates.

musketeer
trooper
offic

uring the Civil War

He also wears a breast plate and a back plate over a coat of thick leather, and has a sword and a musket called a carbine. There would be two pistols on his horse's saddle.

Foot soldiers, or infantrymen, had helmets too. Their pot helmets had brims and a tall comb which made the helmet stronger.

The foot soldiers who used long pikes were called pikemen. They also wore breast plates and back plates. To protect their legs they wore *tassets* which were fixed to the lower edge of the breast plate. A tasset was rather like an armoured apron.

By this time many soldiers were using muskets which fired metal balls by means of gunpowder. These men, called musketeers, did not usually wear any armour. Each one carried his gunpowder in powder flasks which hung from the bandolier. The musket balls were carried in the pouch.

As men began to use gunpowder to fire bullets and cannonballs, wars became quite different. The kind of fighting that you have been reading about began to change, because much of the armour that you have seen could not protect soldiers against bullets.

As guns began to replace the weapons shown in this book, then, so the armour used by soldiers began to go out of use. Men had to think of new ways of protecting themselves.

Try to find out about the guns and other weapons that were invented, and about the forts, block-houses, holes in the ground and armoured tanks that men used, at different times, against such weapons.

INDEX

Printed in Great Britain
at the Alden Press, Oxford
Colour Plates printed by
Compton Printing Ltd, London and Aylesbury
Bound by Kemp Hall Bindery, Oxford